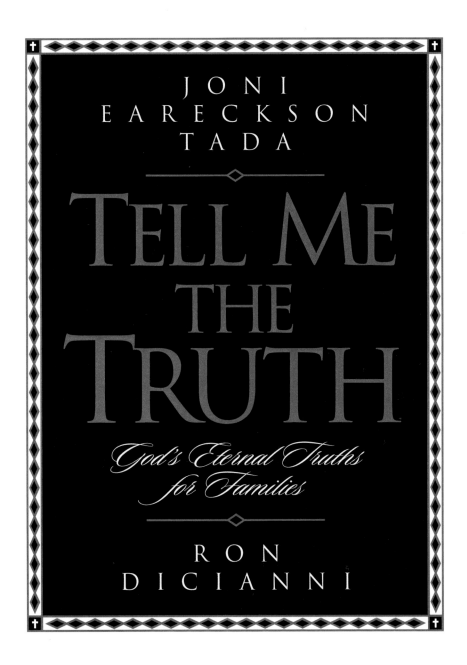

JONI
EARECKSON
TADA

TELL ME
THE
TRUTH

*God's Eternal Truths
for Families*

RON
DICIANNI

CROSSWAY BOOKS · WHEATON, ILLINOIS

A DIVISION OF GOOD NEWS PUBLISHERS

FROM THE AUTHOR

For Kyle Serrano—
my knee-hugging nephew!

◆

FROM THE ARTIST

To Grant and Warren—
the next generation to stand on the Truth.
Hold the banner high . . .

ACKNOWLEDGMENTS

My wheelchair has shown me how much I depend on others. I simply could not do what I do were it not for the kindness of my friends. And so to Steve Jensen, who partnered with me in writing these seven stories, thank you for lending your skills and pressing your heart into this project. Thanks also to Francie Lorey—you have shown patience extra ordinaire in lending me your hands at the computer. Most of all, thank you, Ron DiCianni. Thanks for your heartfelt love for kids. It shows.

JONI EARECKSON TADA

Thanks to Crossway for continuing to believe that these books are mandated in the halls of heaven, Joni and Steve for allowing God to use them again, my family for being as convinced as I am that God has set me apart for this work, and mainly to God for not hiding the Truth from us.

RON DICIANNI

◆

TELL ME THE TRUTH

Copyright © 1997 by Joni Eareckson Tada and Steve Jensen

Published by Crossway Books, a division of Good News Publishers, 1300 Crescent Street, Wheaton, Illinois 60187

Illustrations: Ron DiCianni

Art Direction/Design: Cindy Kiple

First printing 1997 • Printed in the United States of America

Unless otherwise identified, Scripture is taken from the *Everyday Bible, New Century Version*. Copyright © 1987 by Worthy Publishing.

Scripture marked (MESSAGE) is taken from *The Message*, copyright © 1993 by Eugene H. Peterson. Published by NavPress.

LIBRARY OF CONGRESS CATALOGING-IN-PUBLICATION DATA
Tada, Joni Eareckson.
Tell me the truth / written by Joni Eareckson Tada with Steve Jensen ; illustrations by Ron DiCianni.
p.   cm.
Summary: A collection of short stories and paintings which present seven spiritual truths for a Christian life.
1. Christian Life—Juvenile fiction.   2. Children's stories, American.   [1. Christian life—Fiction.   2. Short stories.]
I. Jensen, Steve.   II. DiCianni, Ron, ill.   III. Title.
PZ7.T116Tg 1997   [Fic]—dc21   97-33498
ISBN 0-89107-946-7

05	04	03	02	01	00	99	98	97
15	14	13	12	11	10	9	8	7	6	5	4	3	2	1

A WORD TO PARENTS

Whenever I'm with my sisters and talk turns to childhood days, we agree that our best memories orbit around those sunlit summery days when our family would camp near Rehoboth Beach, Delaware. It was running over sand dunes, splashing in the surf, and steaming clams on the Coleman stove. Then it was hugging our knees around the nighttime campfire on the beach and listening to Daddy tell stories. The blaze made our faces hot and his face bright as he took us on one adventure after another.

No matter where we'd journey, whether sailing the Sargasso Sea or scaling Pike's Peak, whether make-believe or real, Daddy would always weave marvelous truths throughout his stories. Turn the other cheek. Go the extra mile. Forgive seventy times seven. Trust in God. Don't follow the world's ways. "Tell us another one, Daddy," we'd plead long after the last log burned out. I've never forgotten his stories. Nor the truths.

These days most parents don't have the time or opportunity to craft storytelling into a family tradition. Still, when Mom or Dad *is* able to pull up a chair by the bedside and read a "truth-telling" tale, powerful things happen. The story is sealed by the warmth of Mommy's words. The truth is driven home by the smile on Daddy's face. Truth is not imparted to the intellect, but from heart to heart. It shines best when it's conveyed with life and warmth, for truth is a thing not of words, but of life and being—my dad modeled the truth he told around the campfire, and that is why he and his stories still have a powerful and poignant grip on my memory.

This is why I wrote *Tell Me the Truth.* When it comes to reinforcing biblical truths to children in this crazy, fast-paced world, parents need all the help they can get. Steve Jensen and I have composed seven stories that illustrate seven compelling truths from God's Word. You will find these truths laid out on page 49, which you may wish to remove from the book, frame, and hang in your child's room as a constant reminder.

Not only must we hear truth, but also we must respond to it. At the end of each story, your child can affirm his or her understanding of, and belief in, the truth of that story by signing in the place provided. (For more than one child, just make extra lines yourself.)

I picture you sitting by your child's bedside, sharing these stories, and in so doing—sharing your heart. Truth imparted from heart to heart. Truth reinforced by the warmth of your words and the sincerity of your smile. Truth that will last a lifetime. In this spirit I present this book. I think my daddy would be proud of it.

—JONI EARECKSON TADA

THE CLEANSING STREAM

A Shepherd's Choice

---◆---

Everyone who believes that Jesus is the Christ is God's child.

1 JOHN 5:1

ohn Kelvin shielded his eyes to study the scene before him. The tired grass of late autumn covered the hills to his right where the sun was setting. To his left rocky cliffs were turning gold in the last rays of sunlight. Between these two lay a valley with a stream winding southward, passing large oaks along its banks.

He lowered his eyes to see a wave of white move toward him. A herd of sheep was coming home after a day of grazing. Two shepherds rode, one on each side of the herd, and a frantic dog prodded the animals along from the rear.

And they're all mine, John thought.

It had not always been so. The land and the sheep had come to him from his grandfather, who had died earlier in the year. John had visited the farm once as a boy when he came from America for the summer. The old man had no relative in Scotland to take over when he died.

"Come, John," his grandfather's letter had said. "Your father is busy. Tend my sheep, won't you?"

So John had left his dull life in Connecticut and claimed his inheritance.

John now stood watching the lead shepherd approaching him. The man had been a friend of John's grandfather.

"Would you be takin' the herd the rest of the way then, Master John?" he asked.

John hesitated. The sheep stood at restless attention. The dog sat on its hind quarters and panted. The man asked again, this time standing next to John, "I said, would ya like to lead 'em 'ome?"

"I would, Kenneth, but . . . " John looked at the dog. She was a border collie named Nessy. Her black and white fur lay in silky waves. Her nose was streaked with gray. She had been his grandfather's pride and joy—the smartest dog John had ever seen. But . . .

"It's the dog you're worried about then," Kenneth interrupted John's thoughts.

John nodded. "I don't understand it, Kenneth. That dog won't mind my commands."

"Oh, go on. Give it another try," the old man urged.

John shrugged in reply and stepped forward. He stared at the dog, trying to feel that he was in command. He waved his arm forward and to the right in one smooth motion.

The dog did not move, however. She sat straight, staring into the sky. John tried again, but the dog still ignored him. He turned back toward the house in disgust and embarrassment.

"I don't understand it!" he called back at the old man. "I've been here for two months, and that dog is as disobedient as ever. She hates me, I tell you!" He turned back around to press his point. "Everyone else can handle her, but she won't listen to me. I'll find another dog, Kenneth. Mind you, I'll find another dog!"

Kenneth followed John, signaling to the other shepherd to move the herd.

"Ya don't understand," he said as he caught up to John. He stopped for a moment as John turned in anger to hear the explanation. "It's just that the dog, well, she might not know ya own the place."

"Of course I own this place!" John exploded. "My grandfather gave this to me. All of it!"

"Aye, he gave it to you, all legal and such. But try explainin' the law to Nessy."

John was as curious as he was angry. "What'll I do then?" he asked.

Kenneth shook his head slowly. "I don't know, but when you figure it out, she'll com' round for sure."

John turned back toward the house, mumbling to himself. The old man's advice seemed pointless. "There's nothing more I can do. I've tried everything. I'll just get another pup next spring, that's all."

———◆———

John threw himself into the business of the farm that winter. Raising sheep had given his grandfather enough money to live on, but John knew that he could do better. He wanted to double the number of sheep he owned. Within five years, he wanted to be known as the man who made the best wool in all of Scotland.

Despite his dreams, he did not feel the joy his grandfather felt. John remembered the laughter he had heard as his grandfather led the sheep out to pasture. Those strong hands of his gently holding a newborn lamb. And those eyes, those piercing blue eyes, always watching for something in the herd that would signal danger. Yes, John remembered his grandfather and his joy. *Will that joy ever be mine?* he wondered.

———◆———

By early spring John was eager to see his herd grow. He was just as eager to train his new pup. It would be easier to start with a new dog than to figure out what was bothering Nessy. She would do fine for the other shepherds, but he would work with his own dog.

John's plans changed, however. Late one night he woke up from a sound sleep. He thought it was a dream that had awakened him. Then he heard it—the horses screaming in their stalls in the barn. He jumped into his clothes and ran outside. In front of him flames licked at the roof, lighting up the dark sky. Smoke filled the yard. He raced into the flaming building, choking on the smoke. One by one, he began leading the horses out into the field. Soon Kenneth and the others came to help.

"She's burnin' bad!" Kenneth yelled. "Better to let the sheep out of the pens. This fire will spread, and they'll panic! They'll trample each other to death."

John ran to the sheep, Nessy following closely behind. The sheep had indeed started to panic. John opened one end of the pen. Nessy immediately took her place at the rear of the herd without any prompting from John and forced the sheep through the opening. They bolted toward the valley below.

John chased after the herd as they were swallowed up in the darkness. He was surprised at their speed. Only the sound of the dog and the sheep kept him running in the right direction.

As John caught up with the herd, he worried about a new danger. With the stream full from the spring thaw, any sheep that entered the water would be towed under by the current and by the weight of its wool soaked with water.

Nessy had done her best to turn the sheep away from the stream, but when John finally overtook them, three sheep had gone in already. He could see their heads just above the water, straining to keep afloat.

"Stay here, girl!" John yelled at Nessy. He jumped into the icy water and reached the first one in seconds. He grabbed it by the neck and wrestled it back to shore. He turned again and half swam, half ran to the other, a ewe. This animal, too, was heavy and fought furiously with John. It kicked his shins, but he managed to drag this one to safety as well.

John turned once again and raced downstream along the bank to catch the third. But he was too late, as the sheep took water into its lungs. John managed to grab the animal before it went under and pulled it up on the shore. He hoped it would come to, but it did not move. John collapsed beside it, shaking from the cold, and suddenly everything went black.

John awoke late the next morning in his own bed. The shepherds had rescued him, brought him back to the house, and called the doctor. Now with the sun streaming through the window, he felt well enough to get up. He was anxious to see for himself the condition of the sheep, especially the ewes that would soon give birth to their lambs. He hurried out of the house to find the herd.

The barn fire had burned itself out. Only a few wisps of smoke rose from the ashes and the jumble of burned timbers. The shepherds and Nessy had camped around the sheep all night in the valley just below the homestead. Most of the herd was huddled together. A few had wandered off a safe distance to graze. The shepherds walked among them. Nessy sat vigilant.

"Good mornin', Master John," Kenneth greeted him. "You're a fine sight this mornin'."

John nodded with a weak smile. He looked out over the herd carefully. At other times he would have simply glanced over the crowd of wool, but this morning he looked at each one with keen interest. He could not explain it, but somehow he knew these sheep in a different way. He was even able to pick out from the crowd the two he had saved the night before.

"Go on then," Kenneth interrupted. "Lead 'em on 'ome with Nessy. The fire's out now, and they ought to get back."

John looked at Kenneth and then at the dog. She stood as straight as ever, panting and looking into the sky. But this time there was something different in her eyes. Though they still stared ahead, once every other second they darted back to look at John, as if expecting something from him.

He feared failure again, but John raised his stiff arm slowly. He thrust it to his right in the direction of the homestead. Instantly he realized the command he gave did not fit the need of the sheep. The scattered herd was not ready to be moved forward. He cringed at the error.

The dog was not put off by it, however. She sprang into action with such energy that John forgave himself and laughed aloud. Kenneth and the other shepherds laughed heartily as well, watching the dog race to the grazing sheep.

John recovered his senses and began pointing and calling with confidence. Nessy leapt like a year-old puppy at each command, seeming to laugh with the men at each cut and sweep she made.

"What happened?" John asked Kenneth as they watched the dog.

"Ain't it plain to you, Master John?"

John frowned, but then he laughed. His grandfather's friend was playing with him.

"Please, Kenneth. Don't hide it from me. Tell me straight. Why is Nessy doing this?"

Kenneth slapped John on the shoulder. "Why, you're a shepherd now, don't you know?"

"But I've always been a shepherd!"

"Not 'ccording to Nessy. You always owned this place, legal. But not 'til you dove in after those sheep did she see that you loved the sheep the same way your grandfather had. That's the difference now, Master John. You're a shepherd, sure."

John reflected on the old man's words. He knew Kenneth was right. His grandfather had joy because he had chosen to be a shepherd. Instead, John had simply accepted the inheritance as a business, and now he realized that being born into a shepherd's family had not made him a shepherd. He had to choose the life of a shepherd.

He gazed at the herd, the land, the dog—all were no longer just his inheritance. They were, indeed, now the life he had chosen.

"They're really mine," he said softly.

Are you a part of God's family? You may think you are because your parents are. But membership in God's family isn't something you get from your parents—like the shape of your nose or color of your hair.

GOD'S TRUTH IS:

For God loved the world so much that he gave his only Son. God gave his Son so that whoever believes in him may not be lost, but have eternal life.

JOHN 3:16

God wants you to be part of His family. All you need to do is believe that Jesus died on the cross to forgive your sins and then rose from the dead to show that He had the power to save you. If you believe this, you will be a child of God and live with Him forever.

God said it. I believe it.

_____   _____
SIGNED   DATE

NEVER ALONE

Katrina's Song

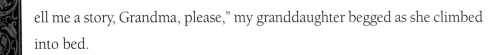

God, we thank you; we thank you because you are near.

PSALM 75:1

Tell me a story, Grandma, please," my granddaughter begged as she climbed into bed.

I smiled and sat down beside her. She was eight years old with long blonde hair, like the color of my hair at her age.

"All right, Katherine," I said. "But listen carefully because it will be unlike other stories you've heard. No dragons. No princes. Agreed?"

She nodded and slid beneath her covers. I breathed deeply and began my tale.

***

Katrina was only thirteen when she found herself working in an open mine in a faraway place called Siberia. Every day she squatted beside a pile of rocks, pounding them one by one until they were no larger than a coin. The work made her small arms sore and her back ache. She wanted to go home.

But she could not. You see, Katrina was in a prison of sorts—a labor camp, they called it. The people the government did not like were sent to such places many years ago. They worked like slaves and lived in crowded cabins with little food and no heat in winter. Most had done nothing wrong. They were good farmers who grew wheat that stood tall in the fields. But someone said that such people were enemies. They were arrested and sent away in the night.

Children did not usually have to go to the labor camps, but Katrina had angered the mayor of her village. This man had sent her father away to Siberia, and so she had stood beneath the mayor's window in the village square. She begged him to bring her father back. She told him how loving her father was and read her dad's poems, poems about the farm, the open sky, and his God.

But the evil mayor hated the truth he heard. Angrily he sent Katrina to a labor camp as well. Her father had been put to work searching for oil. She had to crush rocks that would be used for making roads.

On the 193rd day of her loneliness in the labor camp, Katrina stopped to look at the scene around her. Hundreds of men and women squatted next to their piles of rocks. Their hammers struck like machine guns, piercing her ears. The noise drowned out any memory of home. Of hope. She couldn't stand it any longer.

I am lost, she thought sadly. *God has forgotten me, and I am lost.* Looking up, she wondered, *Where are You, God? Are You lost, too? Have You left me here and can't find Your way back?*

The gray sky gave no answer. She sank to her knees and clung to her hammer, rocking back and forth. "He is lost," she murmured over and over. "He is lost." Then a silent cry came from her heart: *Dear God, if You are here, please give me some sign!*

At that moment, two sparrows landed on a nearby rock. Katrina heard their chirps and watched. They hopped to the ground and ate the tiny crumbs that had dropped from her bread. The birds sang between each bite. Something in the girl stirred at the sound of their music. She remembered a verse in the Bible that said that God watched over every little sparrow. Suddenly she felt better. She wiped her tears, turned toward the sky, and smiled. "You *are* near," she said.

In the cabin that evening, Katrina found a scrap of paper and a piece of charcoal. She shaved the charcoal to a sharp point and began to write in the dim light of an outdoor lamp. She wrote a poem. It was the kind of poem her father would have written if he had been there.

> *"God is lost!" my hammer cried,*
> *"Lost to hatred, lost to pride."*
>
> *But in these fields of heartless stone,*
> *Sparrows sang of hope alone.*
> *They sang their song to train my ear—*
> *"Your God is waiting, waiting near!"*

She held the poem close to her and sighed. Then, like a little girl unable to keep a secret, she looked over the edge of her bunk at the old woman asleep in the bed below. "Wake up. I have a gift for you," Katrina whispered.

The woman awoke and gave Katrina a grumpy look. But she took the piece of paper the girl held out to her. "Jesus is near, you know," Katrina added.

The woman's anger turned to tears as she read the poem. Then she turned to the woman in the bunk beside her. "Read this!" she whispered. "You must read this! Katrina wrote it. Pass it along."

The whole cabin read the poem that night. Some wept softly; others gasped at its simple truth. One started to hum the tune of an old hymn. Before long, another put Katrina's words to the tune. Soon the whole cabin was singing her song over and over again. Their strong voices seemed to split the rafters as the song broke the silence in the camp and filled the air.

The joy did not last long. The words of the poem angered the officials. It was a crime to teach about God, after all. They raided the cabin the next morning and found the poem. Katrina must be punished, they said. Only a prison cell would teach her that there was no God.

They lie, Katrina thought, but she kept silent.

The cell in which they placed her was barely large enough to stand, let alone walk. She had a bed with no mattress and a bowl for her food. A small window near the ceiling let in the only light. She was not to speak to other prisoners or the guards. There would be no whispers in the night. No passing of notes. No tapping on walls to give greetings.

Katrina felt alone. The endless silence killed what little hope she had found when the sparrows had visited her. She could not see the sky to which she had before cried to God. No sounds of rustling leaves calmed her spirit. No warmth from a rising sun touched her skin. Her loneliness gripped her like ice, and she sank into despair.

"I will die," she said. "I will die here alone." Looking up to the ceiling, she cried, "Can You hear me, God? Are You dead, too?"

The gray, cold ceiling of her cell was silent.

"He is dead," she sighed. "He is dead."

The silence continued through the night as Katrina lay awake. Only the morning rounds of the guard delivering bread and soup brought her out of her sad thoughts. She heard him three cells away, then two. She picked up yesterday's empty bowl from the corner. As the guard stopped in front of the trap door of her cell, she bent down. The panel slid open, and a fresh bowl was passed through. She placed her bowl there for the guard to take.

Then a surprising thing happened. Before taking the bowl from Katrina, the guard reached in and touched her hand. It was a light, gentle touch with two fingers brushing against the back of hers. She nearly cried out—she had not been touched for so long. But the door shut, and the guard left before she realized what had happened. She sat on the bed and stared at the door and then at her hand. She thought about that moment of being touched over and over again. As she ate her food, she barely tasted it. Hope had begun to break into Katrina's heart again.

The next morning's delivery of food strengthened her hope even more. Just before the door slid shut, the guard tossed a small package into her cell. It was wrapped in cloth and tied with string. Katrina grabbed it quickly and sat on the bed. She held the package to her chest, fearful that someone might come and take it away. Finally she laid the package on the bed and opened it.

Tears welled up as she looked at what was inside—a pencil and several sheets of paper. She lifted the pencil to smell the wood and stroked her cheek with the paper. She looked up at the window and sighed, remembering the touch of yesterday. Her question to God had been answered. "You *are* alive," she said.

That night Katrina lay awake, adding a new verse to her poem. She tried this word, then that one. Only when she had finished the verse in her mind did she put it on paper. The pale light of dawn was just coming through the window as she wrote.

> *"God is dead," my prison sighs,*
> *"Killed by treason, killed by lies."*
>
> *But through the bars of hopeless steel,*
> *Fingers touched, His love revealed.*
> *They traced the words to forge my will;*
> *"Your God is living, living still."*

As in the labor camp, Katrina could not keep her poem to herself. She folded the paper and waited for the guard to make his rounds. When she heard him outside her cell door, she placed the poem in her empty bowl and passed it through the trap door. He took it without a word.

Katrina wondered during the next several days if she had made a mistake. There were no more gifts, no more gentle touches. She began to fear the worst. Had it been the same guard who picked up her poem? Was all of this simply a trap from the very beginning? As the days passed in silence, Katrina became more and more worried.

It was not until two weeks later that she learned what had happened to her poem. In the middle of the night, a voice from a cell at the end of the hall began to hum. A second soon joined in. And then a third and a fourth. When at last the entire block of cells sounded like a choir, a single prisoner sang out the words to Katrina's poem. Others joined him the second time around, adding strength to the truth of her words.

The guard had not betrayed her after all. He had passed her poem on to the others. Together, they had broken the deadly silence of the prison for everyone. God was indeed alive—and near!

———————◆———————

"The end," I said to Katherine.

She was startled. She sat upright in bed and protested, "But, Grandma, that can't be the end. What happened to Katrina?"

"Oh, that," I said. "The prison guards were certainly upset. But Katrina's punishment didn't last long. She was let out of prison two years later."

"And the guard who was nice to her?" Katherine asked.

"He lost his job. But it didn't matter. He loved Katrina and married her when she was eighteen!"

"And they lived happily ever after?"

"I'm sure they did," I said. "Now get to sleep. It's late." I rose and kissed her. I turned out the light and stood over her until she slept. Then I whispered so as not to awaken her, "Happily ever after, Katherine, yes. But not truly happy until I, Katrina Zhukov, can see my Master face to face. On that day I will hear the last verse of my poem sung by angels."

"God is King," my heart declares,
"King who listens, King who cares."

The darkest night can never hide
My life from Him who's crucified.
I'll teach the angels all to sing,
"My God is faithful—faithful King."

I touched Katherine's hand with my two fingers and left the room. "God is near, my Katherine. God is near."

———————◆———————

There are times that God may feel far away. When bad times come and problems are all around, it may seem that He isn't very close at all. But . . .

GOD'S TRUTH IS:

Be strong and brave. Don't be afraid of them. Don't be frightened. The Lord your God will go with you. He will not leave you or forget you.

DEUTERONOMY 31:6

◆

God said it. I believe it.

_____   _____

GOD IS GOOD

THE WEIGHT OF TWO WORLDS

No test or temptation that comes your way is beyond the course of what others have had to face. All you need to remember is that God will never let you down; he'll never let you be pushed past your limit; he'll always be there to help you come through it.

1 CORINTHIANS 10:13 (MESSAGE)

ever was there a more gorgeous day on Maple Street. The sky was bright and blue, and leaves on the trees rustled in the breeze. It was the perfect day for playing outside. But it wasn't perfect for Benjamin Brewer. That's because Ben felt absolutely stuck in his wheelchair. He sat on his big front porch overlooking the street, leaning his head on his hand and watching kids on the far sidewalk toss a frisbee.

Whoosh! The path of the frisbee went haywire, and it came sailing into the Brewers' front yard. Thump! It hit a tree and fell against the trunk. Benjamin's heart began to race. He straightened in his wheelchair, as if to spring out of it and run for the frisbee. But try as he would, his legs wouldn't move. His shoulders slumped with embarrassment when one of the kids stopped at the edge of the yard and asked, "Can I get my frisbee back?"

Benjamin pretended he hadn't seen it hit the tree. "Huh? Oh, sure, go ahead," he said with a wave of his hand. He then angled his chair away from the boy, who ran into the yard and picked up the frisbee.

The game started again across the street, and Ben turned his chair to watch. Oh, how he wished his legs worked! He looked down at his clean, unscuffed Nikes. *A lot of good a pair of running shoes do me!* he thought. They looked as new now as they did when he got them a year ago. *I hate this stupid wheelchair. I can't do anything. . . . I don't have any friends. It's not fair!*

At that moment, at the other end of the porch (and yet an entire world away), Benjamin was being watched by two angels, Zoe and Astor. Zoe, who was sitting on the railing, shook his head and sighed, "That little guy is carrying the weight of the world on his shoulders."

The other nodded in agreement. Although Zoe and Astor could not feel sadness the same way humans do, it did not take an archangel to see that Benjamin had the blues in a big way.

Finally Astor piped up, "I'm glad the Master sent us here to cheer Ben up. It won't be an easy job. Wheelchairs never are—"

"But," Zoe interrupted as he hopped off the railing and smiled, "that wheelchair will give the Master a chance to show His love and power."

"This I have to see," said Astor. It's not that this angel was doubtful. Indeed Astor had great faith in God. It's just that he didn't know as much as Zoe, the older and more experienced angel who had seen the Master's blueprint for Benjamin's life.

Honka! Honka! It was Tony, Benjamin's next-door neighbor, on his new red bike. Tony made a big figure eight in front of Ben's house. Zoe elbowed Astor. "See that kid? You'd never guess, but he's carrying a lot of weight on his shoulders, too. His dad's away a lot on business. His mother is busy with the new baby. He doesn't play with the other kids. He may look okay on the outside, but he's hurting almost as much as Benjamin on the inside."

"So what do we do with these two boys?" Astor asked. "How do we—ouch!" The angel had leaned against the porch railing. He reached behind him and pulled a nail from the wood. Angels weren't supposed to feel pain like humans, but a heavenly assignment that involved earth had its risks. Astor held the nail up and frowned.

"*This* is how we do it," said Zoe as he took the nail from Astor's hand.

Just then Tony finished his figure eight and called, "Hey, Ben, I'm going to be in the big bike race on Saturday. Wanna come?"

Ben waved back and shouted, "Yeah, maybe I will!"

The two angels could tell from the look on Benjamin's face that he didn't really mean it. Angels could not read the thoughts of humans, but Benjamin's sad smile said it all. They could tell—and maybe even Tony could tell—that Ben *wanted* to go see the neighborhood bike race, but that he'd probably just stay on his front porch.

Zoe sighed at Ben. He sighed at Tony, too, as he watched him wave good-bye and speed down the street. Yes, there was work to do here. The weight of the world on the shoulders of both Tony and Benjamin would get a lot heavier before it would seem lighter.

Meanwhile, as Tony turned the corner from Maple onto Vine Street, he felt suddenly sad. He remembered that this was the exact spot where Ben had been hit by a car two years ago.

He passed this corner hundreds of times without giving Ben's accident a thought. But today was different. He felt deeply troubled that Benjamin could not race a bike the way he could.

Tony stopped for a moment, balancing his bike with his foot against the curb. *I wish I could be a better friend to Benjamin,* he thought, *but how do you play with someone in a wheelchair?* Tony almost turned around, but he felt afraid—afraid that he might be embarrassed and not know what to say, afraid that he might make Benjamin feel bad that he couldn't ride. *Besides,* he thought, *I'm not good at making friends, let alone with a disabled kid.* And so Tony sighed and went on his way.

Astor's face scrunched up in a question. "Why didn't you stop Tony?" he asked.

Zoe shook his head. "I can't make humans do what they don't want to do. But don't worry," he added. "There *is* something we can do."

Saturday morning came and with it all the excitement you'd expect over a neighborhood bike race. A few kids were zooming up and down Maple Street on their bikes, testing their turns and their brakes. Benjamin rolled his wheelchair out onto his front porch before breakfast. Watching everyone do wheelies and figure eights made his eyes fill. He sniffed back tears.

Suddenly from several blocks away, a voice making announcements came over a loudspeaker. The bike race was about to begin. Everyone moved out of the street. Benjamin sighed and started to wheel toward the front door.

Just as he was about to enter the house, he glanced over the side railing of the porch toward Tony's house. Then he gasped. Tony's new red bike was lying on the lawn. And Tony was sitting on his front steps, rubbing his eyes. Benjamin could tell that something was terribly wrong. Forgetting all about breakfast, he wheeled down the ramp by the side of his driveway.

"What's the matter?" he called when he got within shouting distance. "I thought you'd be headed for the starting line with the others."

"My bike tire has a big hole in it," said Tony. Benjamin could tell that Tony also had a big lump in his throat.

"How'd it happen?" Benjamin asked softly as he wheeled closer.

"Who knows? And who cares? My dad is out of town as usual, and Mom says she can't leave the baby to take me to the gas station in time to get it fixed before the race."

Zoe and Astor, who had been listening from their regular spot on the porch, held their breath. This was the big moment. They would now find out if the plan they had put to work last night would succeed.

For the first time in many weeks Benjamin's face broke out into a big, broad smile. "Hey, cheer up," he told Tony. "I know what to do. Follow me!"

Zoe and Astor rubbed their hands together in glee and followed the boys.

A very surprised Tony had to trot to keep up with Ben as they hurried toward the Brewers' garage. Ten minutes later, the two of them were remounting the tire on Tony's bike.

Tony stood back and shook his head in amazement. "I can't believe it's fixed! How did you ever learn to patch a tire so quickly?"

"Aw, it's easy once you've had some practice," said Benjamin. "My wheelchair has a flat every now and then, and because I really depend on it to get me to school and church, the shopping mall, and everywhere else, I need to know how to keep this thing in tip-top shape." He grinned and slapped the armrest of his chair.

Zoe and Astor gaped at each other. Neither angel had ever heard Benjamin say anything so good about his wheelchair. Not in the two years since the accident. Not ever! The angels gave each other a high five.

"Benjamin Brewer, you are really something! You're a regular guy!" said Tony.

"Well, you'd better get moving, or you'll be late for the race. Hey, where is the finish line?"

"In front of the courthouse. Are you coming?"

Ben smiled. "Would I miss watching a friend win a race?"

Astor swung his arm around his fellow angel's shoulder and held up a small object, his face beaming. "Who would have thought a nail from a wooden porch railing would fit so wonderfully into the Master's blueprint for Ben's life?" The nighttime plot to make a hole in a bike tire had worked.

"And not just Benjamin's life," said Zoe. "I think a little weight has lifted off Tony's shoulders, too." The angels stood back and watched to see exactly how the story for both boys would end.

Tony and Ben could hear the final call for the race over the distant loudspeakers. If Tony was going to get to the starting line, he had to rush. But something more powerful than the pull of the race gripped him. He looked at Benjamin, sitting there with grease on his jeans and face, smiling with a wrench in one hand and lug nuts in the other. It didn't seem to matter to Tony that his dad wasn't there or that his mom couldn't leave to watch him. Benjamin could. And that made all the difference.

Tony swung his leg high over the seat of the bike, but then he paused thoughtfully. "You know, it would be great fun to win the race, but I think I've done something more exciting than that already!"

"What's that?" asked Benjamin.

"I've found myself a new friend!"

Ben looked puzzled. "You have . . . Oh! You *have*." He grinned. Ben waved Tony off and stared as the red bike and its passenger turned the corner. It was then that he whispered, "And I have found a new friend, too."

Sometimes problems can pile up so high you're not sure you'll
make it. You may even wonder if God knows what
you're going through—and if He really cares.

GOD'S TRUTH IS:

Let us hold firmly to the hope that we have confessed.
We can trust God to do what he promised.

HEBREWS 10:23

God said it. I believe it.

_____   _____
SIGNED   DATE

THE LIONS' DEN

It's in God's Hands

---◆---

In Christ we were chosen to be God's people. God had already chosen us to be his people, because that is what he wanted. And God is the One who makes everything agree with what he decides and wants.

EPHESIANS 1:11

indsey squirmed against the end of the church pew, trying her best to find a comfortable position. She had sat with her family on this exact bench hundreds of times, but it never felt so hard as it did tonight. Maybe it was because it was a Saturday night missions conference, and she knew she'd be back in the same pew early the next morning. Maybe it was because she didn't like stories about crocodiles, mosquitoes, and snakes. But thirteen-year-old Lindsey had another reason. She was dying to be at the mall with her friends.

"Lindsey," her mother leaned over and whispered, "straighten up."

She huffed and did as she was told. But inside she was still slouching.

After the last missionary speaker left the pulpit, the pianist played a hymn, and Pastor Martin stepped up to make an announcement. "Friends, we've heard some marvelous testimonies this evening from our missionaries on the field. They've sacrificed a great deal to serve God in these foreign countries, and I want us to consider giving a special offering as the plate is passed tonight. Let's pray!"

Lindsey bowed her head and tried her best to pray. She felt guilty she hadn't paid attention to the speakers. She felt guilty that her mind kept wandering to the mall. But she really squirmed when the ushers began passing the plates. Reaching into her pocket, she clutched a five-dollar bill. It was the part of her monthly allowance she had promised her folks she'd give to the missions conference. Lindsey sighed. She would really rather put the five dollars toward the new sweater she had seen at The Gap.

The ushers drew closer. Lindsey squirmed more. Suddenly she cupped her hand and hurriedly whispered to her mother, "I've got to go to the bathroom!" Without really getting permission, she jumped up and escaped out the side door right before the offering plate reached her row.

"Whew! Just in the nick of time!" she said quietly, as she shut the door behind her and leaned against it. From there she walked down the dark hallway to the rest room. She entered, unfolded the bill, and held it up to the mirror. Happy thoughts of a new sweater mixed with feelings of guilt. Lindsey stuffed the bill back into her pocket and decided she'd better get back to the service. The offering plate had surely passed her row by now.

As she was heading up the dark hallway, Lindsey noticed a strange and very bright light streaming from a half-opened door. She peered around it and spied an older man, with a head of wild white hair and horn-rimmed glasses, hunched over a computer. He wore suspenders, a white shirt with sleeves rolled up, and a tweed vest. His jacket hung on the corner of the chair, and several high stacks of thick books were piled on the table. He was typing fast and furiously. Lindsey had never seen anybody the age of her grandparents look so at home with a computer.

"Please do come in, Lindsey," he said without looking up. Lindsey wrinkled her forehead, wondering how he knew her name.

"I'm Mr. Billingsley, and I've been expecting you," he turned and said with a smile.

"Weird," Lindsey murmured, but something about his funny hair and kind smile put her at ease, as though she knew him from the Discovery channel or had seen him in her science book. Lindsey walked slowly into the room and asked, "What are you working on?" like they were old friends.

"Why, this is your Book of Life," he said, patting the nearest stack of books.

This isn't weird; this is way out! she thought, feeling as though she had stepped into one of those silly skits they do up front at vacation Bible school.

Mr. Billingsley smiled and shook his finger. "I can tell you don't believe me, Lindsey. And so, here—" He cracked open one of the books, thumbed through a few pages, straightened his glasses and read: "Date, April 23, 1992. Scene, the lunch table in the elementary school cafeteria. It is Alexandra Kerr's first day at school since moving to the neighborhood. Lindsey Schroeder asks Alexandra to sit with her. Makes big impression on Alexandra, who happens to notice Lindsey's cross around her neck."

Lindsey's mouth dropped open. "How do you know about that?" she asked, disbelieving. "That was six years ago when I was in third grade!"

"Yes, and after her parents moved again two years later, little Alex remembered your thoughtfulness. She also remembered that cross, and so when she was invited to Sunday school, she went. What's more, Alex accepted the Lord Jesus as her Savior. You played a part in that," Mr. Billingsley said warmly.

Lindsey shook her head, as if to wake herself from a dream. She drew closer to the book, placed her hand on it, and decided to test this strange but very nice man at his odd game. She told him about the time she lost her Bible at camp last summer. "What happened to it?" she challenged.

Mr. Billingsley reached for a different book in the pile (explaining that her Book of Life was written in many volumes), flipped it open, and pointed Lindsey to the section that explained the Bible's whereabouts. She read the paragraph, mumbling, "After camp ended, a kid from another church found it under my bunk. He saw all the neat things I had underlined in my Bible . . . made him want to get closer to God. Wow!" she said, looking up. "I remember being so upset that I lost it and that God didn't answer my prayer to find it! This is neat!"

"Now," Mr. Billingsley said, pulling up his chair, "let's get down to business. Would you be in agreement with God as to how He plans for this evening's events to turn out? You do have a say in it, you know."

"I do?" Lindsey asked, puzzled.

"Oh, yes," he said, his hands waiting on the computer keys. "I don't have time to teach a course in God's control and your free will, but you have been, as it says in the Bible, chosen to be one of God's people. And God 'makes everything agree with what he decides and wants.' It's your choice, Lindsey, but God's plan."

This was all too hard for a thirteen-year-old to understand, but Lindsey wasn't about to argue with the Bible or Mr. Billingsley. "So what am I supposed to choose?"

"What you intend to do about Pastor Martin's sermon tonight, of course."

Lindsey had entirely forgotten about his challenge to give money to the missionaries. She fingered the crumpled bill in her pocket. She thought about the offering—and then the sweater. Which would it be? She stalled for time, and asked, "First, can I know how it's all going to turn out?"

"Ho, ho, my dear," Mr. Billingsley chided her, "this isn't Psychic Hot Line. You are the only one who can choose. But I can show you this." He looked up something, turned to his computer, typed quickly, and then punched the "enter" key. Immediately, on the screen appeared the image of a man on the edge of a jungle. It looked hot, and he looked upset. His hands were black with grease. He was holding a wrench and leaning over the open engine hood of a small airplane. Words kept flashing on the bottom of the screen: "Jim Singleton. Missionary pilot. Has prayed for help. Awaiting God's answer."

Lindsey leaned closer to the screen. The jungle pilot was shaking his head, as if he couldn't fix the engine.

"What's this got to do with tonight?" Lindsey asked.

Mr. Billingsley typed in more commands, but the computer kept flashing, "Security Password Required." He leaned back and sighed, "I don't have clearance for the answer to your question. But you definitely have something to do with this pilot. Exactly what, I cannot say." He shook his head and then punched a few keys. Another file popped up on the screen. Mr. Billingsley adjusted his glasses and read the words on the screen. "I can tell here that Jim Singleton desperately needs a high-performance titanium spark plug. The kind that tropical heat and rain won't hurt. Apparently, though, those things are pretty expensive." He then turned to Lindsey. "And, as you heard tonight's speakers say, missionaries aren't rich."

Lindsey clutched the five-dollar bill. "Mr. Billingsley," she said as she began backing away, "can you stay right here? Don't move; don't go anywhere. I've got something to do, and I'll be right back!" She bolted out the door and down the hallway. She slipped in through the side door and slid into her pew, scanning the sanctuary. Lindsey's shoulders slumped. She let out a slow groan. The offering was over, and the plates and ushers were nowhere to be seen.

Her mother noticed the groan. "What's going on?" she asked. "Are you ill?"

"Mom," Lindsey asked urgently, "how much does a titanium airplane spark plug cost?"

Her mother gave her a strange look, thinking for sure a fever had hit her daughter. The service ended, and Lindsey and her family stood to leave. In the shuffle of gathering coats and Bibles, Lindsey made a fast escape to go see Mr. Billingsley. She had to explain that she wanted—*she really wanted*—to help the jungle pilot, but it was too late.

She darted through the hall to the room and then screeched to a halt. Gone was the computer and the books. And sitting in Mr. Billingsley's chair was an elder who, along with several others, was counting the evening offering. "Oh, great," Lindsey shouted, "I'm not too late!"

"Lindsey, what's up?" Elder Johnson asked.

"I want to buy a spark plug. Mr. Billingsley said it was needed right away," she insisted, unfolding the bill and placing it squarely on the table.

"Huh?" He gave her a puzzled look.

"And it's to go directly to help the pilot. Okay?" she pleaded, backing away toward the door. "Can you do that? Please!"

"Okay, okay." Elder Johnson smiled, as though to quiet her down. He reached for the money on the table and gently placed it in the offering plate. "We promise we'll do it, right, gentlemen?" He glanced at the others. They nodded.

Lindsey thanked them all and hurried out of the room.

"Who's Mr. Billingsley?" asked Elder Johnson as he took his pen and marked the amount in his ledger.

At that instant, as his pen wrote, "$5," a clerk in a warehouse thousands of miles away received a phone call, checked his list, and made a few notes on his clipboard. His supervisor signed the forms and yelled to the ground crew at the airport, "Okay, men, load that box that's been waiting. Orders just came down from headquarters. Hurry. The plane's ready to taxi out!"

The ground crew rushed to an airplane waiting on the runway, ready to take off for the jungles of Brazil. They hoisted the box into the open cargo door. The side of the box read: "Handle with Care. High-Performance Spark Plugs."

And at that instant, a pilot leaned on his engine hood to take a break from his work. As he did, he heard the scratchy sound of his air base calling over the radio, "Jim Singleton, come in. We've got those spark plugs coming your way."

The pilot wiped his brow and smiled. *God,* he thought, *is so good. And always in control.*

At that moment, half a world away, a thirteen-year-old, still wondering if she had had a dream, smiled and thought the same. *God is good.* Then she shoved her hands into her empty pockets. *Yes, He is very, very good.*

———————◆———————

Ever think that your decisions don't count and your choices really don't matter? From everything you can see it probably looks that way.

G O D ' S   T R U T H   I S :

Yes, God is working in you to help you to do what pleases him.
Then he gives you the power to do it.

PHILIPPIANS 2:13

◆

God said it. I believe it.

_____   _____
SIGNED   DATE

THE TOUCH

Jesus Is Our Only Hope

Jesus is the only One who can save people. His name is the only power in the world that has been given to save people and we must be saved through him!

ACTS 4:12

unny stepped off the stage, slipped behind the curtain, and pressed her hands against her head. The loud music and the glare of the spotlights gave her one awful headache. The popping of all those flash cameras didn't help either. But that's what she'd come to expect as a top New York fashion model—crowds pushing, cameras flashing, and people always demanding more from her than she could give.

"Hey, Pocahontas! Get changed into your next dress. You're up in two minutes!"

Sunny looked up in anger. Her manager, a large man who wore his gray hair in a ponytail, seemed to think of her as a cartoon character.

Sunny was her name. Actually, it was Morning Sun. She took pride in her Indian blood and in her tribe—the Nez Perce. It was this dark, mysterious beauty—long black hair, brown eyes, and naturally brown skin—that had put her on the cover of at least one magazine a month. But lately even *that* didn't seem to excite her.

Just as Sunny was about to slip into her dress, someone handed her a telegram. It was from Montana, her home state. She unfolded it and read: "Sunny, your Aunt Lily has died. Funeral is Friday. Hope you can come. Signed, your cousin."

Sunny folded up the telegram.

"Pocahontas, you're on!" her manager growled. No time even for sorrow! Sunny threw on her dress and raced for the stage.

Two days later, after five interviews and three photography sessions, Sunny got on a plane heading for Montana. She slumped into the window seat, exhausted. Her eyes were tired and hollow. She was angry at her manager. Angry that her life was so busy. Sunny was just . . . angry.

She stared out the window at the clouds. *I'm even angry at Aunt Lily,* she thought. *Why did she change her Indian name?* Raven Feather was her aunt's name on the reservation. *And my mother—* Sunny choked at the thought of her mom who had died so many, many years ago.

Her mother and Aunt Lily had left the reservation when they started attending a church in town. That's when they changed their names. That's when they made friends with white people. And that's when Sunny's mother became ill—really ill.

Sunny's mom had prayed that Jesus would heal her. Sunny could just barely remember a Bible story about a woman who touched the hem of Jesus' robe. Jesus made the woman in the Bible well, but not Sunny's mother.

After her mom died, Sunny went to live with Aunt Lily. "But I never felt at home with their God," she whispered angrily at the clouds outside the airplane window. "I am Morning Sun, and I will never accept a white man's religion."

Her flight arrived late—too late to go to the funeral. When Sunny got off the plane, her cousin greeted her with a sad smile. Barbara did not have Sunny's beauty. Barbara's face was puffy, and she braided her black hair into tight, short pigtails. *But there's one way she is like my mother and Aunt Lily,* Sunny thought as they hugged. *She still goes to that church!*

"Aunt Lily wanted you to have this," Barbara sighed as she handed Sunny a Bible with some things tucked inside the cover. Sunny opened it and fingered a silver necklace with a tiny mustard seed inside a small, round piece of glass. "I was told the necklace has been in the family a long, long time," her cousin said.

Likely story, Sunny thought. *It's probably something Aunt Lily picked up at one of those religious bookstores.* She unfolded a note on which was scribbled a Bible verse. It was Jesus speaking: "Come to me, all you who are weary and burdened, and I will give you rest." *Sure!* Sunny huffed. *Just like God helped my mother!* She wadded the note up and stuffed it in her pocket. When Sunny caught the hurt look on her cousin's face, she decided she'd better at least wear the necklace.

"Will you come home with us?" Barbara asked.

Home? Sunny thought. Her cousin's house wasn't home. But then again, she couldn't face the idea of catching the next flight back to New York and her too-busy life with its heavy schedule. *"Come to me, all you who are weary and burdened."* The words of Jesus echoed in her mind. She tried to push them out of her head, but something about being in Montana, being almost—home—made her feel lonely. As though she had *no* real home. "No, I can't come with you," Sunny finally sighed. She placed the Bible back in her cousin's hands. "You keep this," she said. "It's not for me."

After her cousin left, Sunny realized she had nowhere to go. She headed for a bathroom to repack some things in her shoulder bag. She looked in the mirror and ran her fingers through her long, smooth hair. She held the little crystal mustard seed necklace. For once, some of the anger inside seemed to drain. "Who am I?" she whispered into the mirror. "I am Morning Sun of the Nez Perce tribe. I am an Indian and—" She broke off and looked around at the women filing in and out. "—and I don't belong here."

Three days later, she arrived in Canada at the old Nez Perce Indian Reservation with a sleeping roll on her back and an unfolded map in her hands. She slid her sunglasses up and shaded her eyes to see what was beyond the gravel road. Morning Sun had come there to find out where she *did* belong. She had decided that the best place to begin to look was in the little trading post at the edge of the road.

A bell jingled when she opened the door. She spotted a shelf of Indian things—feathers and herbs, crystal rocks and little wooden pipes, strange little dolls and tiny totem poles, incense and arrowheads and booklets filled with facts about Indians. Sunny dropped her shoulder bag to leaf through some of the books. She chose the ones that explained the history of her tribe, including the meaning behind the religion of her ancestors. Sunny headed to the cash register and plopped down a pouch full of herbs and crystals. "Are you new to this area?" the man behind the counter asked.

"No," she said, now more sure of herself. "I've come home." With that, she flung her bag over her shoulder and headed for the door, plucking a feather from an Indian headdress and sticking it in her hair as she left.

The next two days she spent exploring the reservation. She went to a garage and asked an old Indian if he knew her family's name. He shook his head. He'd never heard of her great-grandparents or even her grandparents. A couple of Indians sitting outside a market thought they'd heard of them, but they weren't sure. Sunny looked up and down the dirt streets of the small town. A gust of wind kicked up sand, and she held down her flying hair. Picking up her backpack, she headed toward the sunset and the forest beyond the town.

That night, by the light of a crackling fire, she read the booklets about Indians. She read about animal spirits and spirits in the forest. "Hoo-hoo-hoo!" echoed an owl through the trees. Sunny shivered. She started to scoot closer to the fire but jumped when she heard a limb crack in the darkness. She had just learned that totem poles really weren't very nice objects—they were carved images of bad spirits. She went back to reading the booklet, but she couldn't help looking up every once in a while at the bushes around her and the shifting shadows of the campfire. Mumbling a phrase from the book, she reached into the pouch and threw herbs on the fire.

"Whoosh!" the fire exploded. Startled, she dodged away from the licking flames. She rubbed the soot out of her eyes and, exhausted, flopped back on her bedroll. Loneliness came over her like the wall of tall trees. "Oh, Great Spirit, help me!" she cried up at the night, but the only answer was an echo from deep within the forest. Sunny fell asleep.

The next morning she rose, wrapped up her bedroll, and ate a dry muffin. Putting maps and booklets into her shoulder bag, she decided to go back to the trading post. She felt as lonely and empty as ever. Something must be wrong. She didn't belong in New York. She didn't belong in Montana. Looking around at the campsite, she decided she didn't belong here either.

Sunny stared at the embers of her fire. *I thought I'd find happiness in my looks, but I only feel ugly on the inside. I thought it would be cool to be famous and have lots of money, but what a madhouse New York was! I hoped I'd find peace in my people's religion, but the Great Spirit didn't answer.* She sniffed back tears. *What is it I want? Why do I feel so empty?*

Just as she was about to leave the forest, she noticed a small gray church behind several trees some distance from the road. Funny that she hadn't seen it before. Sunny walked over, dropped her things on the wooden steps, and entered. The room was dark and had a wet, musty smell.

She kicked a few pinecones on the floor. It looked as if no one attended this church anymore. *It must be very old*, she thought. She ran her hand over the back of a wooden pew and was about to leave when suddenly rays of sunlight began streaming through the stained-glass windows. The sight made her heart race. It was so beautiful—especially the shades of green and purple in one window. She walked toward it.

She stopped in front of the window, closed her eyes, and let the warm, colorful sunlight wash over her. When she opened her eyes, she saw the stained-glass figure of Jesus with His arms outstretched. He was smiling gently, His hands reaching out in a kind of blessing over two people. One of them appeared to be a missionary. *I remember the man at the trading post telling me about French missionaries coming here,* she thought.

But it was the other person who captured her gaze. It was an Indian woman. Her face was beautiful. *A very familiar face,* Sunny thought as she touched her own cheek. She drew closer to look at a small spot of green light on the Indian woman's neck. Sunny squinted, then gasped. It was a necklace—a small silver necklace with a tiny green mustard seed. The missionary was putting it on the Indian woman.

Tears floated in Sunny's eyes when she saw the soft, accepting smile of the woman who seemed all too familiar—too much like the face of someone in her family. Someone like her grandmother or even great-grandmother. Sunny touched her own mustard seed necklace. *Yes, this has been in the family a long, long time.*

Sunny wiped tears from her eyes so she could read the verse cut in glass at the bottom of the window. "Come to me, all you who are weary and burdened, and I will give you rest." Suddenly she knew that Jesus was speaking these words to her—to her in her loneliness, to her with the crushing weight of a heavy schedule, to her with no place to belong.

She walked up to the stained-glass window and touched the hem of Jesus' garment. "Oh, I am so weary," she said out loud as she leaned her head against the window. "Jesus, help me."

As she waited in silence, peace began to fill her heart. She was no longer alone. Someone was there, and He loved her deeply.

Sunny had found healing for her lonely, sad heart as well as rest for her soul. She had come home.

———◆———

The world will tell you, "You can do it all yourself. Just try
harder. You don't need Jesus to help you out."

G O D ' S   T R U T H   I S :

But the person who trusts in the Lord will be blessed.
The Lord will show him that he can be trusted.

J E R E M I A H   1 7 : 7

◆

God said it. I believe it.

_____   _____
SIGNED   DATE

SPIRITUAL STRENGTH

Chains That Bind Can Be Broken

---◆---

Do not offer the parts of your body to serve sin. Do not use your
bodies as things to do evil with, but offer yourselves to God.
Be like people who have died and now live. . . . Sin
will not be your master, because you are not
under law, but under God's grace.

ROMANS 6:13-14

arcus couldn't remember a time when his chains did not tear into his ankles and wrists, rubbing the skin raw. The chains reminded him of his shame, for he was a slave of the wicked master of the field in which he worked. Marcus had never known freedom. He wasn't even sure what it was. But every once in a while, especially when the west wind blew in, he caught the scent of something fresh and good. He'd breathe deeply and wonder what it would be like to live without chains. That, he decided, would be freedom indeed.

Marcus loved the smell of freedom. It was all he had. For not only was he bound by chains, but he could barely see. More than that, he could hardly hear. It was the same for the other slaves he worked with in the field. What a sad and terrible life they lived!

Suddenly Marcus felt the sting of a whip across his back. It was his master. He felt a shove and a kick. With a groan, he lifted his chains and went back to moving rocks and dirt. Never was there a more tiring job. Marcus and the other slaves worked with heads low. They were not allowed ever to raise their heads for fear that they might catch the scent of freedom when the west wind blew. Their job was also senseless—all they did was move rocks and shovel dirt from one place to the other.

One day when his chains felt especially heavy, Marcus felt an urgent tug in his heart. The west wind was blowing in. He dared to raise his head, drawing in a deep breath of sweet, fresh air. *Yes*, he thought, *it is the beautiful scent of freedom*. Today, however, freedom felt especially close, much nearer than ever before—so near that it seemed as though the figure of freedom was standing next to him. He turned in its direction. Rubbing and blinking his eyes, he thought he saw—yes, he could see!—the blurry form of a boy with no chains on, smiling with eyes sparkling.

"I have come on the wings of the west wind, carrying a message from my master, the King. He has sent me to give you his good news. The news is: 'You shall know the truth, and the truth will set you free.' Do you wish to be free?" the boy asked with a bigger smile. "Do you wish to leave this terrible place and join me in my master's field?"

"Do I wish to be free?" Marcus stammered. He focused his eyes until the image of the boy became sharp and clear. "Of course!" Marcus exclaimed. Not only was he now able to see, but he could actually hear the words sent by the King.

"Then you must leave your chains behind," the boy said.

Marcus looked down. "But I can't," he cried. "I cannot break these chains!"

The boy spoke again, "Know the truth. It will set you free. Come and follow me."

Marcus's heart sank, but he found enough courage to reach for the boy's hand. When he did, to his surprise, his chains unlocked and fell to the ground. With that, the boy grasped Marcus's hand and led him out of the rocky, dirty field, through a gate in a stone wall, and into a lush, green pasture with trees, flowers, and a beautiful brook that flowed from tall mountains in the distance. People were happily working in the fields where corn and wheat were growing. Things grew here! What's more, the pasture smelled heavenly—just like free-dom *should* smell.

Marcus thanked the boy and then turned around to see the happy face of his new master, the King.

"Come into my field prepared for you," the King said. "I am your master, and you will no longer be called a slave, but my friend."

Marcus could hardly believe it! He had been rescued. Saved. Delivered. Best of all, his chains were gone. He rubbed his ankles and wrists in delight. "No more chains—I'm free!" he shouted happily. "I no longer serve that wicked ruler in the old field."

The master of the beautiful pasture smiled and reminded him of one more important fact: "And don't forget, you now have eyes to see the truth and ears to hear my word. Never forget that."

Marcus was glad to see there were others in the pasture. These were free people who had been rescued from the awful field, too. Even the boy who led Marcus out had once been a slave. And like the boy, many free people asked their kind master if they could go back to the old field when the west wind blew so that they could rescue their fellow slaves—just as the boy had rescued Marcus. The kind master always gave them his blessing but warned them to be careful to obey his voice and never to forget the way back through the gate in the stone wall.

One day, after many months of exploring the lush, large pasture, Marcus wandered along the stone wall until he came to the gate. It was the gate through which he had been led into freedom. He became curious. He wondered what was happening on the other side. He looked around. The kind master of the pasture was nowhere in sight. The west wind was not blowing. His friends had gone on a journey to the great mountains. Marcus decided to peek through the gate.

When he did, he heard a frightening sound.

"What are you doing on that side of the stone wall?" a voice growled.

Marcus had never heard the voice before, but he knew at once that this was the voice of his old master—the wicked ruler of the field of dirt and rocks.

"I *said*," the voice bellowed, "what are you doing over there?"

Marcus shivered with fear. Always before he had been deaf and blind to the ways of the old master. Back then he had only obeyed the whip and the kicks and shoves like an animal. But now he realized his old master had a voice—a very powerful and forceful voice.

"Get back in here where you belong!" the wicked ruler snarled. "You don't belong over in that pasture with those people who are free. You belong here. This is where you're supposed to be!"

Marcus's mouth went dry, and his breath came in short gasps. He wanted to turn around, but he froze.

The old master hollered again, "I said, get in here. Now!"

At the word "Now!" Marcus jumped. He stumbled into the field of dirt and rocks and saw for the first time the shape of his evil master—a frightening, huge, strong, dark shape. The old master puffed out his chest. Marcus stooped low, just like he used to with his head down. He looked around and saw the miserable figures of slaves, all of them blind and deaf to his presence.

"I know what you're thinking," the wicked ruler sneered as he swaggered up to Marcus. "You think you're just going to visit here."

Marcus was stunned—that was exactly what he was thinking!

His old master chuckled. "You can forget that idea right now. Here," he said as he threw a set of chains on the ground, "put these on!"

Marcus looked at the chains with heavy cuffs, remembering how they felt against his skin.

Nothing made him see more clearly the horror of life in this terrible place than those dreadful, heavy chains.

The crack of a whip startled him. The wicked master yelled more loudly, "I demand that you put these chains on! Right away!"

The knees of the former slave knocked, and his legs trembled. He felt helpless. He felt he had to obey. He had no other choice. Sadly, he bent over and started putting the cuffs around his wrists.

At that instant a gentle wind touched his face. It was the west wind, carrying the words of the King. The words were faint, much fainter than if he heard them in the beautiful pasture, but Marcus could hear them just the same: "The truth will set you free." Yes, yes, it was the sound of the voice of his wonderful friend—his King, his new master!

The wicked ruler snapped, "That fool has no say over what you do in *this* field. Put on those chains. You're mine!"

Marcus was torn. Why didn't the King come and rescue him? His heart breaking, Marcus cried toward the gate in the stone wall, "Please, come help me. Please, save me!"

But no one came. The west wind blew harder, and the wicked master roared even more loudly.

Again, the words of the King lifted on the breeze: "You shall know the truth, and the truth shall set you free."

"Don't listen to that poppycock!" the angry figure before him warned, holding his whip high, as if to strike.

Just then a light dawned in Marcus's mind. The wicked master had not struck out with his whip. He had not kicked or shoved him like he used to. *In fact,* Marcus realized, *he has not laid a hand on me at all.*

He straightened and raised his head high. His fear left. Now he understood the power behind the words of his friend, the King. Marcus was absolutely free—it didn't look like it, it didn't feel like it, but that didn't change the truth that he *was free*. The words of the King were all he needed. He finally realized that this angry, red-faced ruler had absolutely no power over him. Marcus looked him straight in the eye.

"You are a liar," Marcus said to him, "and you have no right to boss me around. I belong to the King, and my place is in his green pastures."

To Marcus's amazement, the wicked master backed off, like a snake slithering away, like a coward slinking away from the face of courage.

Marcus turned around and walked directly toward the gate in the stone wall, into the good master's open arms. Marcus had almost forgotten how sweet and delightful the King's pasture was. He saw his friends. He saw the boy who had first led him to safely. He breathed in deeply the delightful smell of freedom.

"You must never think that you *have* to obey that old snake," the kind King said softly. Then he sighed with a smile, as if holding back something sad. "But the stone wall cannot keep out the sound of his voice. The west wind, on some days, will be still. Your friends will not always be near you, and even I," the King said warmly, "will not always seem to be near."

Marcus looked deeply into the eyes of his true master and nodded, understanding that these words would help him live the rest of his life in freedom. The King continued, "Believe me when I say that those chains from your old life cannot bind you anymore. Although you can never change back into a slave again, you *do* have the choice to act like one, to live like one. The chains have no power over you—that you do not give them. The power is in what you choose to believe." Tears filled Marcus's eyes—not tears of sadness, but of joy.

"Should you ever be bullied by that miserable master again," the King said, "keep this." He placed a scroll in Marcus's hands.

Marcus slowly unrolled it and read the most powerful and important words of all: "I am the way, the truth, and the life." Marcus looked up into the face of the King.

He realized that if he would remember this truth, he would always be free.

Are there times when you feel tempted to listen to the Devil?
He'll try to convince you to live his way. Don't listen. He only tells lies!

GOD'S TRUTH IS:

*But the Lord is faithful. He will give you strength
and protect you from the Evil One.*

2 THESSALONIANS 3:3

◆

God said it. I believe it.

_____   _____
SIGNED   DATE

FINISHING STRONG

Mrs. Seitler's Order

Let us run the race that is before us and never give up.

HEBREWS 12:1

o one on Staten Island, New York, ever thought Joey Seitler would amount to much when he grew up. He was the slowest, the clumsiest, and the dumbest kid in Mr. Rowan's sixth grade class. No one ever picked him for anything—teams, class projects, games. Everyone thought he was a loser.

But a trip to the delicatessen in 1942 changed all that. It was his mom who started it all.

"Here's an envelope, Joey," she said. "Take it to Mr. Baumeister at Armor's German Delicatessen on 7th Street. Inside is my order and some money. My note says it's very urgent because our family is going to the Jersey shore tomorrow to celebrate your sister's birthday."

"At Asbury Park?"

"Yes, that's right. I'm asking him to make submarine sandwiches that we can pick up on the way," she said as she sealed the envelope. "Now don't let this message out of your sight. Like they say in the army, you've got your orders!"

Joey took the envelope in his hand and ran out of the house. He got only as far as the alley before trouble started. Billy Burdock, the toughest kid in school, stepped out of the shadows and blocked Joey's way.

"What ya got, little man?" he growled.

"Nothin'," Joey answered, clutching the envelope tightly.

"Then give me your nothin'," Billy ordered as he grabbed Joey's small hands and took the envelope away. Smiling, he tore the envelope in half and studied the contents.

"Nothin' in this half," he said as he tossed it to the ground. He looked into the other half, and his face broke into a big smile. "Whoa! Three bucks! Now this I can use." Billy laughed at Joey and slipped back into the alley with the money and the other half of the envelope. "Thanks a lot, little man," he called.

Joey stared down the alley. Then he picked up the half of the envelope that lay on the sidewalk. Peering inside, he saw only half of a torn letter. Most kids would have turned around at this point and gone home. But Joey was stubborn. He had his orders, after all, just as his mom said. *I've got to deliver this no matter what,* he encouraged himself. *I made a promise.*

After walking for half an hour, however, Joey wasn't so sure he had made the right choice. Things didn't look familiar. He stopped at Wescot Boulevard and realized that he was lost. He stood dazed and confused.

"You lost, young fellow?" a voice came from behind. It was an old man.

Joey nearly broke into tears. He couldn't answer.

"Where are you going?" the old man tried again.

Joey could only answer by handing over the torn envelope with half of the address.

"The 7th Street Armory. Well, you're not far from it. Just walk two blocks straight ahead, turn right, and then you'll see it. There's a guard at the front, I think. I'm sure you'll like the guns and tanks they keep there," the old man said as he walked away.

Baumeister
7th St. Armor
URGENT

Joey was puzzled by this last comment but followed the directions anyway. He arrived at the armory a few minutes later. The building was huge, with two cannons on the lawn and barbed wire fencing all around. A guard with a rifle stood out front, just as the old man had said. Joey approached him.

"Beat it, kid!" the soldier barked before Joey had a chance to say anything. "No one gets past me without orders!"

Joey looked at the envelope in his hand. He remembered his promise to his mom.

"But I've got an order—right here," he said. "I'm supposed to deliver it to Mr. Baumeister."

The private changed his tone of voice. "Why didn't you say so in the first place? Go on in. You'll find him on the course."

Joey entered the building and found a sign that pointed to a large field outside. Obstacle Course, it said. He followed it and found himself facing a large wall with ropes hanging from the top. He could hear a man shouting at other men behind it. *Must be Mr. Baumeister,* he thought.

The only way to get to the man, it seemed, was to climb the wall. Though he would never have completed the task at school, the thought of his mission gave him new strength. No scary wall would prevent him from keeping his promise. He climbed to the top in less than a minute. Down below he saw a huge man chewing a cigar, still yelling at the others. He looked up at Joey.

"What do you want, kid?"

"I've got a message for you, Mr. Baumeister," Joey said as he caught his breath. "The guard told me I could find you on the course."

The man laughed. "You've got the wrong guy. I'm Sgt. Williams," he replied. "You want Col. Baumeister on the golf course." He pointed to green hills in the distance. "Head that way and through a fence. You'll find him there."

Joey thanked the sergeant and climbed back down. Within a few minutes he found himself in front of four men about to play golf. "Mr. Baumeister?" Joey ventured.

A tall man stepped forward.

"Well, it's about time you got here, caddy! We almost had to tee off without you. Next time don't be late. Here, hold my bag!" He thrust the bag full of clubs at Joey.

"But I—" Joey started to say.

The colonel held up his hand. "No talking! My golf caddies don't talk. Got it?"

"But—"

"No buts. Let's go."

And so Joey followed, hauling a forty-pound bag of clubs through the entire course. He chased the colonel's bad shots into woods and creeks. He washed the little white balls at the start of each hole. He even fetched water for everyone to drink. *I'm not sure a few sandwiches are worth all this work,* he thought. Then he remembered his promise to his mother. *But Mom's counting on me. I can't quit.* He picked up the bag and trudged on.

Finally after eighteen holes of bad golf, Joey was allowed to speak. "I've got a message for you," he said as he handed over the envelope. The colonel took it and sat down at a table under an umbrella.

"Don't expect a big tip," he warned. He unfolded the letter, read it once, then twice. Then he exploded out of his chair. "Where did you get this?"

Joey winced. "From—"

"Never mind!" the colonel interrupted. "We have to act on this right away." The officer turned to his golfing partners. "Men, get my jeep—now!"

They all ran for the parking lot. Joey stood alone with the colonel, pleased. He had worried that the order might not be filled, but this Baumeister was certainly a man of action.

"Sir," Joey said as calmly and as firmly as he could, "I don't know where you're taking that letter, but I'm not supposed to let it out of my sight. Those are my orders, and I made a promise."

The colonel stared back at Joey and thought for a moment. "You're right," he said. "We need more than this letter. We need the boy who delivered it. You." Tapping on Joey's chest, he added, "And you probably know more about this than what's in the note, don't you?"

Joey nodded as he thought of the money. "Yes, sir, I do."

"I thought so. Now, tell you what, you and I are going on a plane ride." He turned to the men in the jeep. "Call ahead to get a plane ready. We're going to the Pentagon."

"In Washington, D.C.?" one of them asked.

"No, in Brooklyn!" the colonel yelled sarcastically. "Of course in Washington. Now get my plane ready!"

Two hours later, Joey and the colonel mounted the steps of the Pentagon where all the big shots in the army worked. A military police officer led them to the top floor. "The general is in the briefing room waiting for you," he told them as he opened the door. Joey and the colonel entered a room and were met by a small man. He was somewhat bald with large ears and a big smile. The colonel saluted.

"At ease, Henry," the general said. "Now what's this big news, and why is this boy with you?"

"This will explain everything, sir," the colonel said as he placed the half-torn letter on the table. The general put on his glasses and read the letter.

Suddenly the general slammed his fist on the table. "I can't believe it! Hitler's made a big mistake if he thinks he can come this close to our shores!"

"Wait, it's not—" Joey tried to stop the general, but the man was too angry to listen. The officer grabbed a phone and dialed a number.

> URGENT
> New Jersey shore tomorrow
> at Asbury Park
> fastest German
> submarine
> pick up the package
> 9:00 a.m.
> itler

"Sherm? This is Ike. Listen. A message from Germany has fallen into our hands. I want your crews patrolling the waters off Asbury Park. Keep your eyes open for a German sub. They're planning to come in tomorrow and pick up a package. Get your boats there immediately."

"But—" Joey tried again as the general got off the phone.

"Listen, young man. I don't know who you are or where you came from, but if we find a sub in those waters tomorrow, you'll be a hero! And someday you could be a general in my army!"

◆———◆———◆

Believe it or not, Joey *was* a hero. Turns out there really was a German submarine off the coast of New Jersey the next morning. The newspaper headlines read, "Local Boy Helps Capture German Sub." They even had a parade.

And Joey did grow up to be a general, but not in the army. You see, Joey was so good at delivering that message that everyone told him he ought to be a mailman. So that's what he did. He spent his whole life not giving up as he delivered things for people. "I make a promise to people, and I don't quit," he always said. And he was so good at keeping that promise that he ended up being the Postmaster General of the whole country!

How do I know all this? Well, I hate to admit it, but I'm Billy Burdock—the bully, remember? And Joey's my boss now. I do errands for him and type his letters. It ain't bad working for him though. He's a nice boss. Once every year, in fact, he takes me to lunch, and we celebrate the day he captured the Germans. Then after we eat and talk about old times, we each take out our part of that famous letter. We lay them side by side on the table.

And then we have a big laugh over Mrs. Seitler's order.

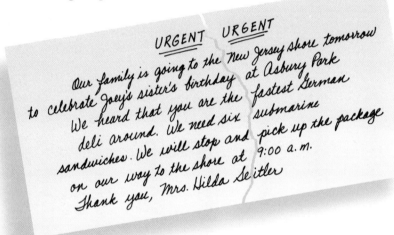

URGENT   URGENT

Our family is going to the New Jersey shore tomorrow to celebrate Joey's sister's birthday at Asbury Park. We heard that you are the fastest German deli around. We need six submarine sandwiches. We will stop and pick up the package on our way to the shore at 9:00 a.m.
Thank you, Mrs. Hilda Seitler

Is the race getting long? Is being a Christian getting harder for you, not easier? Do you think it would be easier just to give up?

G O D ' S   T R U T H   I S :

God began doing a good work in you. And he will continue it until it is finished when Jesus Christ comes again. I am sure of that.

PHILIPPIANS 1:6

◆

God said it. I believe it.

_____   _____
SIGNED   DATE

ARTIST'S NOTES

THE CLEANSING STREAM (PAGE 4)

Many of us (including myself) have met Christ at a church altar. However, you can ask Christ to come into your heart at home, in your seat at church, or away on vacation. Anywhere you are when you recognize that there is only one way to heaven and a right relationship with God, you can experience "the cleansing stream."

In the painting I use a waterfall emanating from the cross in the stained-glass window to represent the cleansing stream Jesus spoke of in John 7:38. We receive this cleansing when we repent, accept the atoning work of Calvary, and ask Christ to be the Savior and Lord of our lives. There is no other way to obtain it. Not through heredity. Not through association. Only by personal experience. At the "altar."

NEVER ALONE (PAGE 10)

One afternoon several years ago my wife and I with our three-year-old son were picking up our older son after school. As we walked out of the building, our little one decided to blaze ahead. To my concern, he headed straight between the cars for the lane of traffic.

Within seconds, my worst nightmare unfolded before my eyes. I saw that Warren was on a collision course with a car coming in an obvious hurry. My heart stopped. I watched as Warren *ran* right to the edge of inevitable danger with too much momentum to stop or reverse. Then as though a giant hand formed a wall between him and the oncoming car, my son not only stopped, but he actually *bounced backwards.* I didn't see any angels, just the result of their presence. Warren is living proof of Psalm 34:7: "The angel of the Lord encamps around those who fear him, and he delivers them."

This painting dramatically depicts God's promise of protection. The boy lazily makes his way home from school, possibly through a shortcut that he really shouldn't take. It's late in the day, and the sun is beginning to fade. There may be danger; however, the mighty angel God has assigned to him is more than enough to guide him home.

GOD IS GOOD (PAGE 16)

As I am writing this, my thoughts are reeling from one of the most difficult weeks I have had in years. I encountered uncertainty, unwelcome changes, broken relationships, and I made several whopping mistakes. I find myself asking: Is God still here with me?

Last Sunday my pastor's sermon was titled, "When You Feel God Has Forsaken You . . ." It was appropriate in light of what happened to me this week. I asked myself while driving my son to school (life goes on, you know) if God is still good even when He doesn't seem to be.

I left last Sunday's service with great expectation that God would reveal in some way that He is always with me. What happened was the opposite of what I expected. But you know what? The result was the same. God proved, through it all, that I did not slip through His tender fingers into a giant black hole where He couldn't shelter me. I *felt* that I had. But the truth is, He made sure that I didn't get more than He knew I could bear. It was more than I wanted to bear, just not more than I *could* bear. I think that's His promise, if I remember correctly (1 Cor. 10:13).

IN THE LIONS' DEN (PAGE 22)

In the process of executing this painting, I actually photographed a 700-pound male lion named Brutus. He was brought to the studio by a zookeeper and professional trainer. I never realized how incredibly powerful a lion is when you see it close up—with no bars between. As his trainer held the chain, it seemed that he was leading Brutus. But all Brutus had to do was move his head slightly in any direction, and his "master" followed, like it or not.

Imagine Daniel's situation. Hungry, savage lions were his sleep-over hosts. In a sense, he was invited for dinner. Was Daniel afraid? Did he wonder how far God was going to let this go, or did he know all along how the story would end?

At times it is appropriate to be concerned and even scared. God understands. He knows how we are made. That's the time to remind ourselves that God wants our trust, and in return we get His help.

The modern "Daniel" represented here has a look of concern on his face, and his body language demonstrates it—rightly so, as the eating machine stares at him. What he doesn't see yet is that God has sent an angel to protect him. The angel and the chains holding the lions are invisible but effective. You might detect a slight smile on the angel's face. That was intentional.

THE TOUCH (PAGE 28)

Many of us have heard that God cares and that He answers prayer. We have heard testimonies of His help in time of need. For each of us, though, the only testimony that really counts is—our personal one. Is He here in *my* time of need?

A woman in the Bible had the chance one day to form her own opinion. Granted, she wasn't in a position to wait and see. She needed help, and she needed it right away. The Gospel of Luke indicates that she had tried everything else first. Twelve years' worth. Possibly the money was gone, along with her hope that her problem would ever be resolved.

Evidently Jesus' reputation must have gone ahead of Him to her town. Could He help her? Should she take a risk? She was touching the hem of a rabbi's robe, and she was unclean. That would have been a huge mistake if she had been caught. When you get desperate though, reason goes out the window, along with pride. Her daring act paid big dividends. Read Luke 8:43.

The woman in my painting is modern, symbolizing our questioning generation. She reaches right past the fancy garments to the one who had the real power—Jesus—the one who still has it today. You will find out for yourself when you need to reach for His hem, too.

SPIRITUAL STRENGTH (PAGE 34)

I grew up in the inner city where the strong dominated the weak. It was my ambition to someday grow big enough to wield the power. On the way I found Christ and discovered that I was misguided. Violence complicates situations rather than solves problems. It's harder to build a house than to tear one down.

Sometimes I still fall back on the idea that force gets you to the finish line faster. Why be patient and soft-spoken when you can yell and threaten to get your way? After all, isn't it the Rambos and karate experts who win in the movies?

Samson was the "Rocky" of his day. Although he made a great start as one set apart for God, somewhere along the way he lost it. Even knowing that his strength came from God, he must have concluded that he could break God's commands and still succeed.

In this painting, look where violence got Samson. He was broken, forsaken, and imprisoned, working like a beast at a mill. He even had to depend on a young boy to quench his thirst. Notice the shadow falling on the grinding wheel—Satan laughing. You see, the whole time Satan knew where reliance on the physical would lead.

Note: Resolve to think God's way. We have God's Word so that we can learn from the mistakes of those who have gone before (1 Cor. 10:11).

FINISHING STRONG (PAGE 40)

Remember the story of the race between the tortoise and the hare? It seemed an obvious mismatch—the strong, seemingly invincible hare against the slow, methodical tortoise. Here we see the danger of overconfidence and distractions.

The Christian life is a marathon—not a sprint. We can't pray for a day and have it last forever. Daily we have to come back to the table to be nourished. We need to build the spiritual disciplines into our lifestyles. That doesn't sound as exciting as one mountaintop experience, but it is more lasting. That's the point.

The apostle Paul gave us a model: "I have finished the race, I have kept the faith. Finally, there is laid up for me the crown of righteousness" (2 Tim. 4:7–8). Determine to be one who makes it to the finish line.

OTHER BOOKS IN THE SERIES

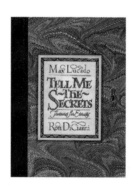

For more information on the art of Ron DiCianni
visit his web site at www.art2see.com

I AM THE WAY AND THE TRUTH AND THE LIFE *John 1*

YOU SHALL KNOW THE TRUTH AND THE TRUTH WILL SET YOU FREE *John 8:32*

TRUTHS THAT SET YOU FREE

God makes you his child when you accept Jesus as your *Saviour*

God is *always* with you

God only gives you what you can *handle*

God is in control of your life to carry out *His* plan

God is your only *Hope*

God has set you *free* from the evil one

God helps you to live faithfully for *Him* until the end